COLD CASE CLOSED

Using Science to Crack Cold Cases

CHERITON
CHILDREN'S BOOKS

Published in 2023 by **Cheriton Children's Books**
1 Bank Drive West, Shrewsbury, Shropshire, SY3 9DJ, UK

© 2023 Cheriton Children's Books

First Edition

Author: Sarah Eason
Designer: Paul Myerscough
Editor: Louisa Simmons
Proofreader: Ella Hammond

Picture credits: Cover: Shutterstock/Koshkina Tatiana; Inside: p1: Shutterstock/
Felipe Caparros; p4: Shutterstock/Andrew Angelov; p5: Shutterstock/Kitreel; p6:
Shutterstock/Couperfield; p7t: Wikimedia Commons/Fallout Boy; pp8-9: Shutterstock/
Couperfield; p9: Shutterstock/Trambler58; p10: Shutterstock/Corepics VOF; p11:
Shutterstock/Stephen Barnes; p12: Shutterstock/Maksim Shmeljov; p13: Shutterstock/
Jaroslav Noska; p14: Shutterstock/Ground Picture; p15: Shutterstock/Felipe Caparros;
p16: Shutterstock/LiliGraphie; p17: Wikimedia Commons/Federal Bureau of
Investigation; pp18-19: Shutterstock/Ronnachai Parkeethong; p19: Shutterstock/Have
a nice day Photo; p20: Shutterstock/Couperfield; p22: Shutterstock/Gorodenkoff;
p23: Shutterstock/Couperfield; p24: Shutterstock/Couperfield; p25: Shutterstock/
PressLab; pp26-27: Shutterstock/M Hazwan H; p27: Shutterstock/Ragne Kabanova;
p28: Shutterstock/Lia Koltyrina; p29: Shutterstock/Mouii; p30: Shutterstock/Microgen;
p31: Shutterstock/Felipe Caparros; p32: Shutterstock/Maksim Shmeljov; p33:
Dreamstime/Tossi66; p34: Shutterstock/Gorodenkoff; pp36-37: Shutterstock/Billion
Photos; p37: Shutterstock/M Bonotto; p38: Shutterstock/Podyom; p39: Wikimedia
Commons/Richard Buckley, Mathew Morris, Jo Appleby, Turi King, Deirdre O'Sullivan,
Lin Foxhall; p41: Shutterstock/Peppinuzzo; p42: Shutterstock/Gorodenkoff; p43:
Shutterstock/PeopleImages/Yuri A; p44: Shutterstock/Koshkina Tatiana.

Printed in China

Please visit our website,
www.cheritonchildrensbooks.com
to see more of our high-quality books.

CONTENTS

CRACKING COLD CASES

Cracking a case is rarely easy for crime investigators. Crime-solving is complicated, painstaking, and often difficult work. While most crime detective series and movies show a conclusion to each case, the frustrating truth is many crimes cannot be solved. These tough-to-crack mysteries are called "cold cases," and they can remain unsolved for years, or even indefinitely. However, thanks to major advances in science and technology, more and more difficult and previously unsolvable cases are cracked every year.

Old Case, New Science

When detectives are investigating a criminal case, if the case cannot be solved, it is kept "on file." If new **evidence** is found, or new techniques are developed that can then be used to retest existing evidence, the case will be reopened. In recent years, many cold cases have been reopened and evidence has been reexamined using new crime-science techniques. The techniques have helped **convict** many criminals for crimes that they **committed** years ago.

Before a case is classified as "cold," every piece of evidence associated with it will be carefully studied.

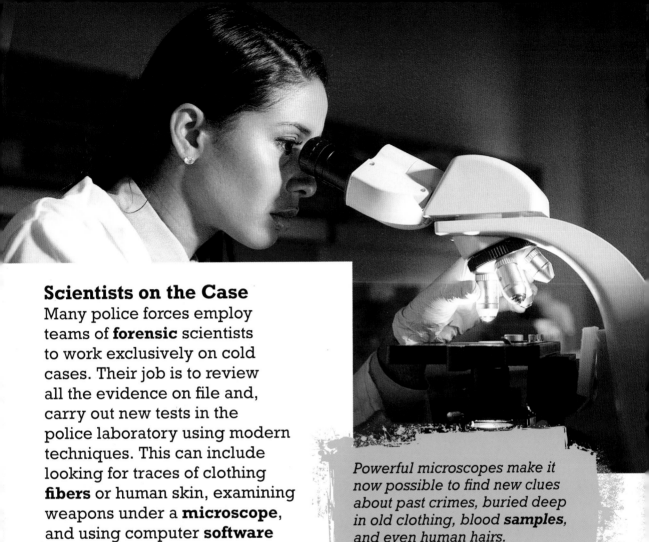

Scientists on the Case

Many police forces employ teams of **forensic** scientists to work exclusively on cold cases. Their job is to review all the evidence on file and, carry out new tests in the police laboratory using modern techniques. This can include looking for traces of clothing **fibers** or human skin, examining weapons under a **microscope**, and using computer **software** to figure out the exact angle a bullet entered a **victim**'s body.

*Powerful microscopes make it now possible to find new clues about past crimes, buried deep in old clothing, blood **samples**, and even human hairs.*

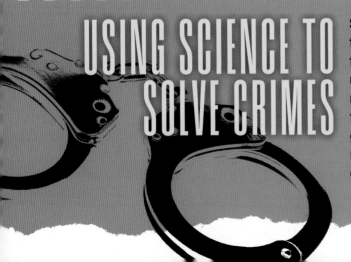

USING SCIENCE TO SOLVE CRIMES

Science is vital to the teams trying to crack cold cases. There are many forensic science techniques that can be used to reexamine old evidence, and new science is being developed all the time. Using forensic science will not get results in every case, but detectives now stand a much greater chance of closing mysterious cold cases.

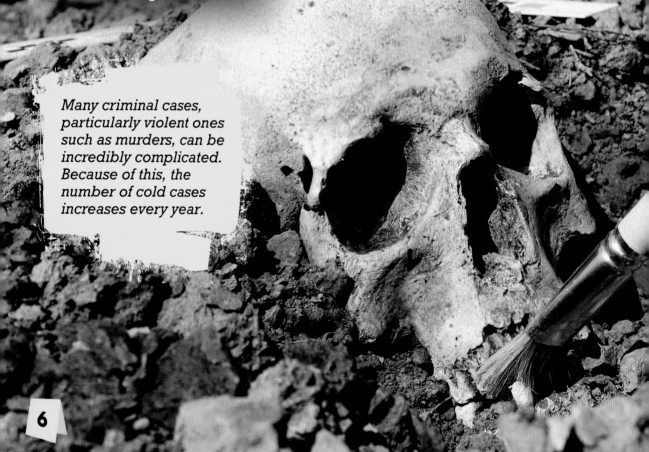

Before Forensics

Many cold cases that are reopened today are historic, meaning that they happened many years ago, before using forensic science as a crime-fighting tool really began. The idea of using forensic science techniques to crack crimes is new in the field of crime detection. It is only in recent decades that sophisticated forensic science methods have begun to be used in crime investigations. Before then, detectives had to rely on traditional methods of police work, which included interviewing **witnesses**, taking crime-scene photographs, and searching for evidence.

Cold Without Forensics

In some cases, traditional police methods were enough to crack the case. However, there were plenty of times when traditional techniques did not deliver results. For example, police still have unsolved murder cases on file that went cold decades ago due to a lack of strong evidence. Without the scientific techniques needed to examine the tiniest piece of evidence, in many cases, detectives had little to go on.

Many criminal cases, particularly violent ones such as murders, can be incredibly complicated. Because of this, the number of cold cases increases every year.

TRUE CRIME STORY

Even high-**profile** cases involving multiple homicides, or murders, can remain unsolved. One of the most famous examples is that of the "Zodiac Killer," who murdered at least four women in California between 1968 and 1970. Despite the police receiving letters from the killer, various tip-offs, and huge interest from the public, the Zodiac Killer has never been identified. It is unlikely he will ever be caught, even though the California Department of Justice has kept the case open for more than 50 years.

The "Zodiac Killer" gave away few clues, other than a logo that he used to sign his letters. The case is one of the most famous unsolved murder cases in the United States.

Never Cracked

According to the Center for the Resolution of Unsolved Crimes, there are hundreds of thousands of violent crimes in the United States that remain on file as cold cases. The Center estimates that since 1980, there have been more than 185,000 unsolved murder cases. Unfortunately, some of these are unsuitable for reexamination using modern scientific techniques because of lack of evidence.

FIND THE FINGERPRINTS

In the past, forensic science techniques were limited, but one of the most widely used was fingerprint **analysis**. In fact, this forensic science technique has been used by crime investigators for more than 100 years.

Printed Clues

If you look at the tips of your fingers, you will notice patterns of lines and rings, called friction ridges. Every person's friction ridges are slightly different, so their fingerprints are also different. When a person touches something, they leave behind a fingerprint that is unique, and can be used to **identify** them.

Different Prints

There are three types of fingerprints. The first is a three-dimensional (3–D) plastic print, which is left on soft surfaces such as soap or wet paint. The second is a print that is made on a hard surface, such as a wall, when blood, dirt, or another substance is transferred from a person's finger onto the surface. The print is visible and is called a patent print. The third is a print that is made when sweat or oil from a person's body is transferred onto a surface via their fingers. The print is invisible and is called a latent print. Latent prints are discovered by dusting a surface with fingerprint powder, which then shows up any prints.

Collect and Match

Forensic investigators collect patent prints by photographing them. Latent prints can also be photographed and lifted from a surface using a clear tape. Plastic prints left in an object such as a bar of soap can be removed from the crime scene, or photographed. Once crime-scene prints have been collected, they are scanned and the digital images are run through a computer **database** system, to see if they match with any prints on the system. If there is a match, crime investigators decide how to take the investigation forward.

Crime Science

A new machine has breathed new life into the age-old technique of fingerprinting. The machine, nicknamed CERA, uses electricity and ceramic powder to reveal previously hidden fingerprints on metal surfaces, such as bullets and guns. Hopes are that it will help solve cold cases that have, until now, proven hard to crack.

Latent fingerprints can be left on surfaces such as glass.

CHAPTER 2

SOLVING THE PAST

Forensic science has been the turning point in cracking cold cases, and developments over the last decades have meant that many forensic-science techniques have been advanced, perfected, or invented. That has allowed the police to reexamine cold cases with new eyes.

Gory Work

Detectives working on cases of violent crimes, such as murders and attacks, always pay close attention to any blood-splatter patterns found at the crime scene. This is because the location and patterns of blood, for example, on walls, floors, and clothing, can reveal a lot about exactly how the crime was committed. Today, bloodstain analysis is one of the essential forensic tools.

Crime scenes are carefully photographed so that the images can be later analyzed by crime investigators.

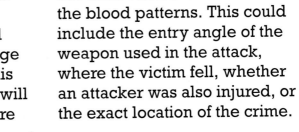

Blood found at a crime scene can provide vital clues.

Blood in Motion

Bloodstain analysis is quite complicated, but the basic techniques used are easy to understand. For example, the length and width of a bloodstain pattern can reveal how far the blood fell before hitting a surface, and even the angle of entry of the weapon used in the attack. To help bloodstain analysis, crime scientists take detailed photographs and video footage of each crime scene. Once this is done, a bloodstain analyst will examine them to try and figure out what can be learned from the blood patterns. This could include the entry angle of the weapon used in the attack, where the victim fell, whether an attacker was also injured, or the exact location of the crime.

CRIME SCIENCE

In the past, techniques for analyzing bloodstains were limited. Today, scientists understand a lot more about blood and why it makes the patterns it does when it hits a surface. Bloodstain analysts use computer software to create an accurate 3-D animation to show detectives how the blood ended up where it did. These animations are based on crime-scene photographs, so they are of great use in cold cases, in which old photos can be reexamined.

11

Ballistic Breakthroughs

Another key forensic method regularly used by crime scientists on cold cases is called ballistics. This is the scientific examination of firearms, or guns, bullets, and gunpowder. Ballistics is as important in solving cold cases as it is in regular crimes.

Looking for Clues

Once a weapon has been found or recovered from a **suspect**, close analysis can help scientists figure out in what crimes the weapon was used. It may be that scratch marks inside the barrel of a gun link it to an unsolved crime. It is also possible that tiny traces of gunpowder **residue** found at a crime scene many years ago may also be found on or within the suspect's weapon. Ballistics analysis can tell scientists a lot about how crimes were committed.

Investigators scour a crime scene to find any bullets that may have entered surfaces.

Gun crime is so widespread that many police departments have their own firearms laboratories. These are places where forensic scientists can test weapons and examine them under microscopes. In these test centers, investigators carefully examine guns and bullets connected to unsolved crimes.

Joining the Dots

One of the major ballistic discoveries of recent years is ballistic fingerprinting. This is the process of matching a bullet to a specific gun. When a gun is fired, **microscopic** scratch marks are left on both the bullet and the barrel of the firearm. These marks are unique to each bullet and weapon, making them a great way of linking a gun to a crime.

Scratch marks have been left on this bullet. Scientifically analyzing clues such as this can be vital in solving crimes.

For around 100 years, crime-scene photography has been a crucial part in solving crimes. Today, it is more important than ever, because powerful computer programs are now available to crime investigators.

The programs allow crime scientists to examine images incredibly carefully, so even the tiniest clues are not missed.

Crimes Magnified

Today, most photographs are taken digitally, so they can easily be stored and transferred between computers. It is also easy to digitize old photographs so they too can be stored on computers. In the past, detectives looking at crime-scene photos had to use a **magnifying** glass to check minor details. Software programs now make it possible to magnify images to hundreds of times their original size.

Investigators study highly magnified crime-scene photographs so that any vital clue is picked up.

For many years, investigators were puzzled by the case of Nicholas Lori, an 11-year-old boy who had been found dead, but without a clear cause. Police suspected his parents of killing their child, and for 15 years after Nicholas's death, they were the chief suspects in the case. However, the parents were cleared of any wrongdoing when new image software became available to investigators. It was used to examine the original case photographs, and confirm that Nicholas had been killed by a dog, not his parents.

Closing in on Clues

In order to reexamine old photos using computer software, scientists must first create an accurate digital copy of the original photo. This is done using a machine called a scanner. The scanner recreates the photo as a series of tiny dots and squares, which are called pixels. The smaller the dots and squares are, the more accurate the copy. By making a "high resolution" copy, with at least 300 tiny dots per inch (DPI), crime scientists can zoom in on tiny, potentially case-cracking details in the image without the photograph becoming blurred.

By reexamining crime-scene photos using modern software, scientists may find previously missed evidence.

All in the Detail

Along with old photographs, other documents such as typed or handwritten letters can also now be reexamined and analyzed using modern scientific techniques. Investigators call this forensic document analysis.

True or False

Forensic document analysis is often used to prove the **validity** of key documents in criminal cases, and sometimes their **origin**. It is also used to detect **forged** documents, such as passports and drivers' licenses. In the past, it has been used to solve many fraud cases, for example, when someone tricked a person or company out of money, but is increasingly used in criminal cases involving handwritten notes or letters left by criminals.

Clues in Words

Handwriting analysis is a tricky science, but it has proven very important in a number of cold cases. When comparing examples of handwriting, document examiners look in detail not just at how words are written, but also at the space between them and the pen strokes used by the writer. They also look at the way sentences are structured and the type of words used by the author.

The shape of letters, how smooth and dark the lines are, and the space between letters, words, and lines can provide many clues about the author of the handwriting.

TRUE CRIME STORY

One famous case that was solved using handwriting analysis is that of the Unabomber. In 1978, a package exploded at Northwestern University in Illinois. Over the next 16 years, a series of similar bombings took place, injuring many people and killing three. In most cases, the bomb was sent in the US mail, and the unknown bomber became known as the Unabomber.

Federal Bureau of Investigation (FBI) analysis of the packages showed that the bomber went to great lengths to cover his tracks. He avoided using materials that could be traced, such as store-bought glue, instead making his own glue. But he did leave one piece of evidence—his handwriting. The Unabomber sent letters about his crimes to the police and media, and using handwriting analysis, investigators were able to pinpoint the age of the writer and where he might be. That led to the arrest of Ted Kaczybski, and the closing of this long-running cold case.

When Ted Kaczybski was finally tracked down, the criminal was discovered hiding out in a cabin in Montana.

TEST FOR TOXINS

Crime shows on television often focus on the results of toxicology tests. It makes exciting viewing, but in real life, the tests are a vital part of crime-solving. Toxicology tests are used to show if the deceased swallowed or injected something dangerous, such as drugs, alcohol, or poison, in the days or weeks leading up to their death.

Reasons for Testing

When performing toxicology, a scientist has three main aims. The first is to discover if a substance may have caused harm or death. The second is to establish if the substance could have changed the person's behavior or judgment. The third is to find out if there is good reason why the substance is in the body, for example, because it is a drug prescribed by a doctor.

Clues in Bodies

In cold cases, toxicology can offer rare and vital clues to the detectives handling the case. If samples of blood or human hair are kept in storage, they can be retested using the latest techniques. Traces of certain drugs and poisons, for example, remain in human hair for many months or years, and by studying the contents of someone's blood, urine, or stomach, it is possible to detect different types of drugs and poisons.

Suspicious Searches

Drugs and poisons often change form once inside the body, so toxicology is a complicated process. To help them, toxicologists often use a machine called a spectrometer. This separates a blood or urine sample into its component chemical elements. If there is something suspicious in the sample, however small the amount, the spectrometer will find it.

Crime Science

Some forensic scientists are carrying out virtual **autopsies**. These are bloodless autopsies that use high-tech software to analyze a body and convert each layer of soft tissue into a 3-D **simulation**. The investigator can then inspect each part of the body without ever needing to pick up a **scalpel**. It means the autopsy can be carried out remotely, or not in the same place as the body, and the body need not be **disfigured**.

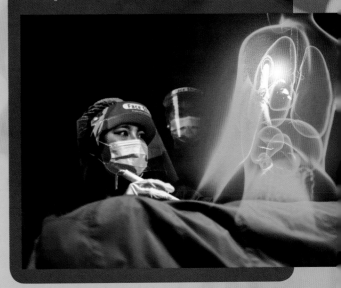

Virtual autopsies could revolutionize crime investigation. They will make it possible for forensic experts around the world to have access to autopsies and provide their opinions as the procedures take place.

CHAPTER 3

NO STONE UNTURNED

Over the years, many criminal investigations have ground to a halt because of a lack of evidence. Sometimes, though, the evidence is there but goes unnoticed. This is when taking a second look for evidence, sometimes years or even decades later, can get results.

At a crime scene, it is vitally important that found evidence is carefully marked out—even the position of the evidence itself may later help explain how a crime has been committed.

Looking Again

The police have to deal with so many cases that sometimes a crime with little clear evidence may be forgotten, or simply go unattended for years. Then, out of the blue, the police may get a new tip-off that reignites the case and leads to a conviction.

Tiny Evidence, Big Breakthroughs

Using many of today's leading forensic techniques, crime scientists can find previously hidden clues in the tiniest pieces of evidence, from shreds of fabric and a few tiny pieces of cotton to what looks like specks of dust. In years gone by, it would have been impossible to see this evidence, let alone test it. Today, forensic scientists have the tools to take old evidence out of storage, reexamine it, and make breakthroughs. In cold cases, a conviction is still rare. Usually, if a cold case is going to be solved years after the crime took place, it will be by reexamining old evidence using cutting-edge forensic science techniques that have recently become available.

TRUE CRIME STORY

The murder of Nancy Marie Bennallack had been a cold case for nearly 52 years until it was finally cracked in 2019. Nancy was killed in her apartment in Sacramento in 1970. For years, investigators tried to solve the crime, but failed. Then, in 2019, new DNA **genealogy** testing resolved the case. The police had long-suspected that a man named Richard John Davis, who lived in an apartment near Nancy's, could be her murderer. When the genealogy testing became available, detectives decided to try and use it. They contacted a relative of Davis, who agreed to giving a DNA sample. Investigators were able to link it to DNA found at the crime scene, thereby determining that Davis must have been the killer. Although Davis had died in 1997, confirming that he was the killer finally closed the long-standing cold case and gave the victim's family some closure.

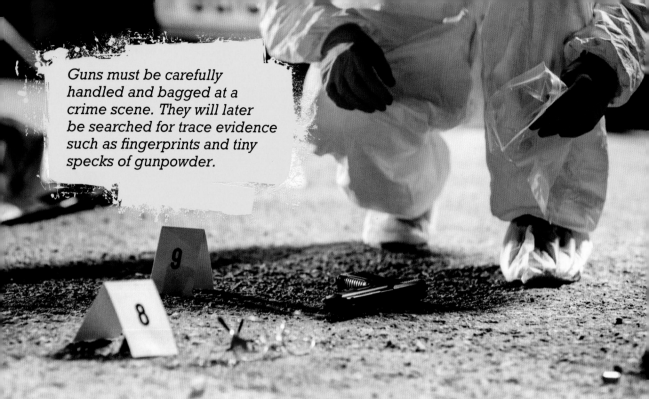

Guns must be carefully handled and bagged at a crime scene. They will later be searched for trace evidence such as fingerprints and tiny specks of gunpowder.

Hidden Clues

It is now routine for crime scientists working on cold cases to reexamine original evidence using powerful microscopes. Microscopes may reveal many new clues, from specks of gunshot residue and tiny spots of blood to hidden fingerprints and rubber from the sole of a criminal's shoe. These minute clues are called trace evidence, and analysis of them is known as trace-evidence analysis. What is discovered can give cold-case detectives vital new clues about a case.

Clues in Contact

Trace evidence is evidence left at a crime scene when two or more objects come into contact with each other. Sometimes, the contact is big enough for detectives to see. For example, marks left by a ladder skidding across a stone floor, the flecks of paintwork removed when someone brushes against a wall, or a torn piece of fabric from a criminal's clothing are all easily seen. Trace evidence can also include glass, hair, fibers, soil, and cosmetics. Not all trace evidence is visible to the human eye. That is why the evidence is examined using a microscope, which makes it possible to discover many new and important clues.

When a gun is fired, microscopic pieces of gunpowder dust are released into the air. These often settle on nearby objects or clothing. To find them, trace analysts must use a scanning electron microscope. This powerful tool allows scientists to look at objects that are 500,000 times too small for the naked human eye to see.

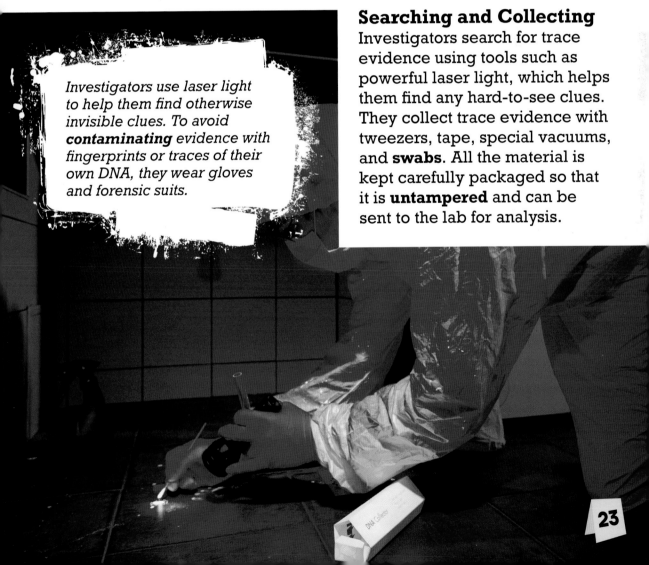

*Investigators use laser light to help them find otherwise invisible clues. To avoid **contaminating** evidence with fingerprints or traces of their own DNA, they wear gloves and forensic suits.*

Searching and Collecting

Investigators search for trace evidence using tools such as powerful laser light, which helps them find any hard-to-see clues. They collect trace evidence with tweezers, tape, special vacuums, and **swabs**. All the material is kept carefully packaged so that it is **untampered** and can be sent to the lab for analysis.

23

Clothes Crack Cases

One of the greatest uses of modern trace analysis is for looking in detail at clothing worn by crime victims and criminal suspects. Using the same methods as those used to detect gunshot residue, crime scientists can find vital new clues that are hidden deep in the fibers of clothes.

Following the Threads

If you look at any type of clothing under a powerful microscope, you will see that it is made up of many individual threads of fabric, woven together to make one garment. As tiny parts of these individual threads can come loose in contact, a criminal could **unwittingly** leave them on the body of a victim. By examining evidence under a microscope, crime scientists may find clothing fibers.

Forensics and Fibers

The fibers of clothing may hold other clues that can be used in a cold-case investigation. For example, tiny amounts of gunshot residue could be buried in the weave of a sweater, coat, or T-shirt. It is also possible that evidence of human hairs or skin flakes could be caught in the victim's or suspect's clothing. In some rare cases, crime scientists have also found microscopic spots of human blood on clothing fibers.

Crime scenes are carefully sectioned off to avoid people entering them and disturbing important trace evidence.

Trace evidence is often too small to be easily seen. Scientists search every inch of a crime scene to find it.

TRUE CRIME STORY

When sisters Kati and Kristin Lisk mysteriously disappeared in Virginia, they were just 12 and 15 years old. Five days later, their bodies were found in an area of forest. There were no witnesses or evidence to explain what had happened. However, there were a few tiny pink fibers on Kati's body. The hunt to find who was responsible began, but the case went cold.

Six years later, a 15-year-old girl was kidnapped in Columbia. She was taken to an apartment, but managed to escape and lead police back to the building. There, the police found the body of the girl's kidnapper, Richard Mark Evonitz—he had killed himself. They also found a linen trunk containing a pink bath rug. When the fibers were checked, they matched those found on Kati's body. Kati's fingerprints were also found on the trunk. It was clear that Evonitz was the killer, and the case was finally closed.

EXHUME FOR EVIDENCE

If all other methods have been tried and there is no other alternative to cracking a cold case, detectives can ask to reexamine a body, even if it has been buried for years. That means removing the body from its burial place, which is called exhuming. This extreme course of action is not taken lightly, but can be the difference between cracking a case and letting it go unsolved.

Buried Poison

There are many reasons why a body could be dug up and reexamined. For example, on original examination, a death may have been attributed to natural causes, but new evidence suggests that foul play could have been involved. With today's advanced toxicology tests, it is possible to discover tiny amounts of **lethal** poison in a body many years after death. If cold-case detectives suspect poisoning, they may have little alternative but to **exhume** a body from its grave. Forensic science techniques are now so advanced that even the smallest samples of body parts can be tested for poisoning.

Crime Science

It is also sometimes necessary to look for trace evidence that may have been overlooked in past investigations. **Pollen** from plants or seeds from grass may point to where a crime took place, for example, but these clues can only be found by reexamining the body, searching for the trace clues, and analyzing them using new forensic techniques. Today, pollen **biomarkers** are being used to link people with murder sites and weapons long after a crime took place.

Who Is It?

The other main reason for exhuming a body is to try and identify it. There are many examples of homicide victims who have been buried, following rigorous but unsuccessful attempts to identify them. Identification of bodies is now much easier because of the development of accurate **deoxyribonucleic acid (DNA)** tests. Thanks to DNA, more cold cases are being solved than ever before.

*In rare and unusual cases, police may ask the family's **permission** to exhume a body in order to carry out new forensic tests. The samples taken are sent to the laboratory for analysis.*

CHAPTER 4

DNA DETECTIVES

The single greatest tool in the forensic toolbox is DNA profiling. This is the process of using human DNA to identify individuals. Since the first DNA profile was made in England in 1984, the technique has revolutionized crime science, and led to countless cold cases being cracked.

Passing It On

To understand the significance of DNA, we must first understand what DNA is and how it works. All living creatures pass on their features to their descendants using **genes**. We get some of our genes from our mothers, and some from our fathers. Crucially, everybody's genes are slightly different, though they may share some similarities with their parents. Every one of the 100 trillion **cells** that make up the human body contains our genes, collected together as DNA. Our DNA is like the body's instruction manual and identification kit rolled into one. It tells us how to grow, how to repair ourselves, even how to think. It can also identify us.

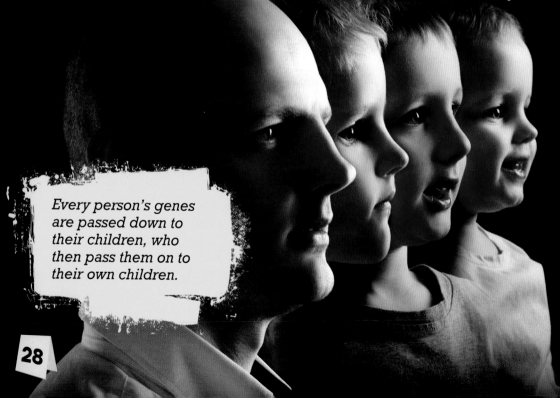

Every person's genes are passed down to their children, who then pass them on to their own children.

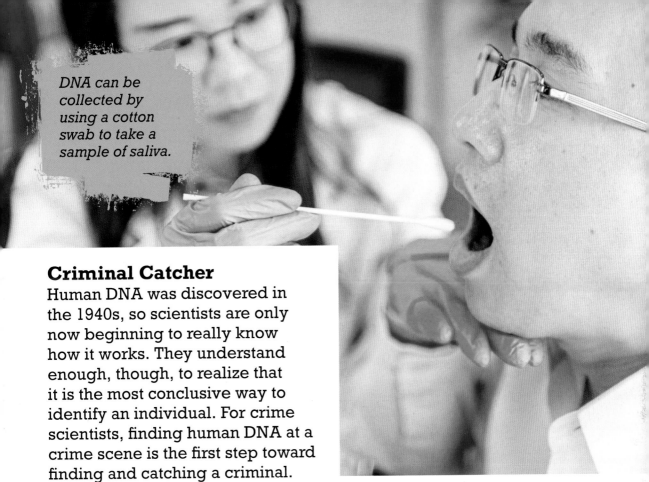

DNA can be collected by using a cotton swab to take a sample of saliva.

Criminal Catcher

Human DNA was discovered in the 1940s, so scientists are only now beginning to really know how it works. They understand enough, though, to realize that it is the most conclusive way to identify an individual. For crime scientists, finding human DNA at a crime scene is the first step toward finding and catching a criminal.

TRUE CRIME STORY

Many cold cases have been solved thanks to matching DNA discovered at a crime scene with that of a suspect. Eighteen years ago, Krystal Beslanowitch was killed in Utah with a blow to her head. The granite rock used to make the blow was kept while the case remained unsolved. In 2013, new forensic technology made it possible for investigators to take **touch DNA** from the rock using a tool called a forensic vacuum. The DNA was matched with Joseph Michael Simpson, a bus driver who lived in Utah at the time Krystal was killed. Simpson was finally tracked down, 18 years after the crime had been committed.

Crime scene investigators take small samples of evidence that may contain DNA and put it in a sterile container. It is then sent to a laboratory where it is tested.

Profiling the Past

In 1984, a scientist working at a university revealed a new way of cataloging human DNA. From this, he was able to create a test that could be used to make an accurate DNA profile of any individual. Today, DNA profiling is invaluable to crime scientists.

Because human DNA is found in every single body cell, it can be found in a wide variety of substances. DNA is present in blood, hair, skin, nails, and saliva. If a criminal came into contact with their victim or other objects scattered around the crime scene, it is likely that they left behind some traces of DNA. For example, a criminal may leave sweat on surfaces that they touch and saliva on the side of a glass or cup that they drink from. Even skin cells from the criminal can be transferred onto an object or a person if touched.

DNA Clincher

If someone is arrested during a criminal investigation, it is likely that a sample of their DNA will be taken so that it can be compared with any traces of DNA found at the crime scene. Many criminals have been convicted on the basis of a confirmed DNA-profile match. The technique has also allowed cold case investigators to reexamine old evidence to see if any traces of DNA can be found. If so, it gives the investigators a positive lead. All they have to do then is match the DNA with a suspect to try and close the case.

CRIME SCIENCE

There are various methods of extracting DNA samples. One of the most advanced is **mitochondrial** DNA analysis. Unlike standard DNA analysis, which takes samples from liquids such as saliva, blood, and sweat, and soft tissues such as skin, mitochondrial analysis is used to make up DNA profiles using bones and teeth.

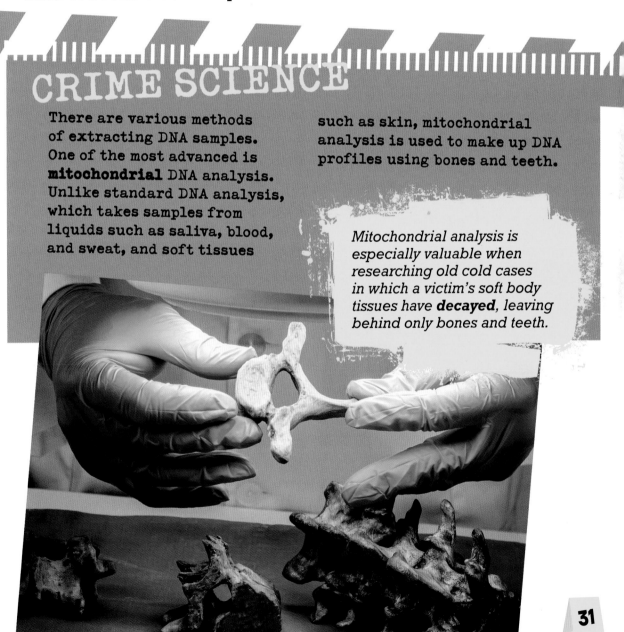

*Mitochondrial analysis is especially valuable when researching old cold cases in which a victim's soft body tissues have **decayed**, leaving behind only bones and teeth.*

Database of Clues

In recent years, it has become common for the police to take DNA samples from suspects and convicted criminals. The samples are then passed to scientists, who test them. The scientists are known as DNA analysts. After testing the DNA, they make up a DNA profile. That is then entered into and stored on a national DNA database, which can be used when DNA is found at a crime scene in the future.

DNA Catalog

In the United States, the national DNA database is called the Combined DNA Index System (CODIS). It was established by the FBI in 1998, and in 2007 held more than 7 million DNA profiles on file. When investigating crimes, detectives will regularly check DNA samples found at crime scenes against records held in the CODIS database. If a match is found, this is known as a "cold hit." Such cold hits often identify suspects. However, on their own, they are not a guarantee of guilt.

DNA databases have made the process of matching suspects with a crime scene far quicker and more likely.

CRIME SCENE DO NOT CROSS   CRIME SCE

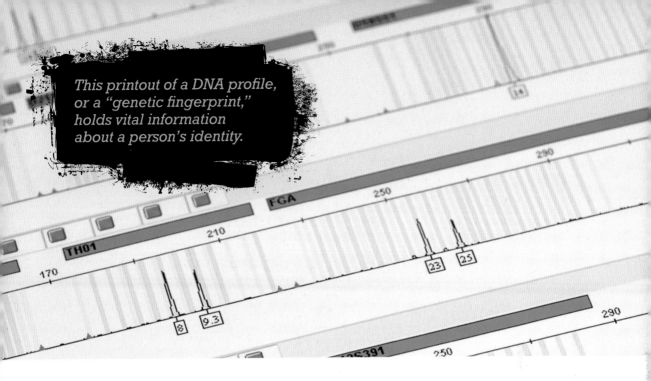

This printout of a DNA profile, or a "genetic fingerprint," holds vital information about a person's identity.

Cold Hits for Cold Cases

The CODIS database is also useful for detectives investigating cold cases. When a cold case is reopened, evidence will be reexamined and cross-referenced with the CODIS database. Many historic cold cases have been solved by doing this.

TRUE CRIME STORY

The CODIS database helped close the cold case of Dusty Myriah Shuck, who was murdered in 2006 in New Mexico. Detectives searched for evidence at the scene, but found little.

In 2022, a man named Garry Artman was identified in relation to the death of another woman in Michigan. He was arrested and his DNA collected. The DNA was uploaded to CODIS, and a match between Artman and the DNA found on Dusty's body was made.

DNA Isn't Perfect

There is no doubt that modern DNA profiling techniques have had a huge impact on the way crime scientists work. They have also helped solve some of the world's most famous cold cases. However, on its own, a DNA-profile match may still not be enough to convict a suspect.

Not Enough Proof

Even if a suspect's DNA is found at a crime scene, it is not necessarily proof of guilt. In some criminal trials, suspects have successfully argued that their DNA has been present at the scene for another reason. Some have also argued that the DNA evidence has been tampered with or contaminated.

This means that the DNA samples have not been kept properly or securely, and there is a chance that they have been mixed up or confused with other samples.

Fake DNA

The police have also become increasingly worried about the possibility of "fake DNA" being left at crime scenes, or given by suspects in blood tests. In 1992, one suspect—a doctor who was accused of attacking unconscious patients—tried to trick blood testers by inserting a tube full of another person's blood into his arm. The trick worked three times before police eventually found a DNA match.

Some suspected criminals have argued in court that DNA evidence is not as accurate as people think. Unless evidence is very securely bagged and handled carefully when it is examined, it can be contaminated.

Doubting DNA

Nobody knows exactly how accurate DNA evidence is. Scientists say that it is 99.9 percent accurate, but critics claim there are flaws in the system. They say that there is roughly a 1 in 100,000 chance that a DNA match will be wrong. While that is still a very small chance, it demonstrates that DNA profiling can never be perfect on every occasion. Despite the doubts of some, DNA profiling is easily the most accurate method of identification crime scientists have to date.

FIND THE FAMILY

Sometimes, it is impossible for crime scientists to find an exact match using DNA databases such as CODIS. However, all hope is not lost—it can be possible to trace a criminal by concentrating on "familial DNA." Familial DNA is the genetic traits shared by all the members of a family.

Gene Generations

Although everybody's DNA is unique, DNA of members of the same extended family will be similar. This is because a percentage of genes are passed down through generations. The DNA of brothers, sisters, and cousins, for example, will share similar traits. In cases where no exact DNA-profile match can be found, crime scientists will search for a partial match or family match. If a family match can be found, it helps narrow down their search.

Narrow It Down

When searching for familial DNA matches, crime scientists use a special piece of software that narrows down the search to a set of agreed genetic traits. What they are searching for are specific genes that are likely to be unique to the family of the criminal they are investigating. The first US criminal caught using this method was Luis Jaimes-Tinajero, who was arrested in 2008 for breaking into cars. Police initially found no exact match, but noticed that DNA obtained from blood samples found at the car crime scenes bore a similarity to the DNA records of Jaimes-Tinajero's brother, and from that important clue they were able to link his brother Luis to the stolen cars, and arrest him.

Crime Science

Although it is clear that familial DNA can be very useful in helping solve difficult cases, many states are reluctant to use the cutting-edge forensic tool in their crime investigations. At present, just a few states use the technique. That is because the science is so new very few laws and guidelines about its use exist, which makes organizations reluctant to use it. Another concern is that it could lead to unfair investigations of people based upon crimes their relatives committed.

DNA was the missing link in the car crimes that were committed by Louis Jaimes-Tinajero, and has also been the tool in linking suspects with crimes in similar cold cases.

History Rewritten

Using modern forensic techniques to look at old cold cases can bring great results. However, it can also work to the advantage of those wrongly convicted of crimes they did not commit. DNA evidence, in particular, is helping solve many historical mysteries.

Finding the Missing

Every year, millions of people around the world go missing. Some are never found, and their families suffer the agony of not knowing whether they are dead or alive. Every year, bodies are also found, which police are unable to identify. Today, crime scientists and DNA analysts use DNA profiling to try and identify these unknown bodies.

Mitochondrial DNA will prove invaluable when trying to solve cold cases, such as war crimes committed during the war in Ukraine.

TRUE CRIME STORY

In July 2012, **archaeologists** in Leicester, England, began a search to finally crack a 500-year-old mystery. They believed they had at last discovered the grave of King Richard III. The king was killed in battle in 1485, and his body was then mutilated and buried secretly. Despite many years of searching, it was never found. Then, in September 2012, a skeleton was discovered in a parking lot. The skeleton was removed and examined, and using DNA testing, shown to be the former King of England.

Scientists finally identified the body of Richard III using DNA examination.

Murder and Mitochondria

On a number of occasions, crime scientists have been able to identify cold-case murder victims using mitochondrial DNA testing of their bones or teeth, many years after they died. For example, when a young woman was reported missing in Anchorage, Alaska, her mother gave FBI officers a saliva sample to help them with their investigations.

The mitochondrial DNA was entered into the FBI's National Missing Person DNA Database. Years later, hikers discovered the **decomposed** remains of a body in Alaska. The body was tested for DNA, and it matched that of the mother. Tragically, the woman was likely murdered, but at least being able to quickly identify her body concluded the investigation into what had happened to her.

Right a Wrong

Over the years, many people have gone to jail for crimes they did not commit. Today, these people have been given a chance to prove their innocence thanks to recent advances in forensic science.

Police Mistakes

In the years before thorough scientific testing was used by criminal investigators, detectives had to rely on witnesses and basic police work to prove that a suspect was guilty. While these methods may have helped lead to the conviction of true criminals, they also sometimes led to innocent people going to jail. Before the use of forensic science, the only hope these people had of proving their innocence was either showing that the police made mistakes or the rare discovery of new evidence.

Case Reopened

Today, in the United States, people convicted before forensic tests came into use can appeal to a judge to have the evidence in their cases reexamined. If this appeal is granted, crime scientists will carefully examine all evidence using modern forensic tools. On a number of occasions, this kind of forensic reexamination has proven that people are innocent and that the police made mistakes. When this happens, what was thought to be a "solved" crime suddenly becomes a cold case, and police must reopen the investigation to try and find the true criminal.

TRUE CRIME STORY

In 1979, Gary Dotson was convicted of attacking and kidnapping his girlfriend. He said he was innocent, but his girlfriend insisted that he was guilty. In 1987, his former girlfriend admitted that she had lied in court. In 1989, new DNA tests on original case evidence finally proved that Dotson was indeed innocent. He was the first person in the United States to be cleared of a crime using DNA evidence. Since his case, improved DNA testing has helped free a number of people who have been wrongly convicted and imprisoned for crimes they did not commit.

Due to the accuracy of modern DNA tests, today, fewer innocent people are sent to prison. However, mistakes are sometimes still made.

THE FUTURE OF COLD CASES

In recent decades, crime science has undergone a major revolution. It has gone from being a small, underfunded area to becoming the backbone of modern police work. Crucially, it has also helped crack thousands of unsolved mysteries.

Cold-Case Policing

In the days before the forensic-science revolution, most cold cases were never solved. When all leads were exhausted, the investigation would quietly close. More often than not, the case files would be put in storage, never to be looked at again. Now, with the development of high-quality DNA testing, trace analysis, toxicology, and other forensic methods, many police forces have their own cold-case teams that can focus on trying to solve historic mysteries.

Forensic investigation is time-consuming and intricate, but it can be the key to solving a cold case.

More Crimes Cracked

Despite the advances in crime science, not all mysteries can be solved. Sometimes, there is little evidence to reexamine, or DNA testing is simply inconclusive. DNA can be matched only if the person is already a suspect, or the government has the person's DNA on file. Yet, as crime science continues to evolve, and new techniques are invented, more criminals will be brought to justice for their past crimes, and more cold cases will be closed. And as techniques improve and more criminals are caught soon after a crime is committed, the number of cold cases will shrink.

MAKE CRIME SCIENCE YOUR FUTURE

Working in forensic investigation requires a lot of dedication and hard work. Investigators must be able to think sharply and leave no stone unturned as they examine crimes. If you think you have what it takes to work in this cutting-edge science field, overleaf you'll find a career guide that could help you one day crack cold cases.

COULD YOU CRACK COLD CASES?

Crime dramas win record viewings, and these gripping shows have inspired many to enter the world of crime science and investigation. It is an amazingly exciting field to work in, with new, game-changing developments emerging all the time.

However, crime dramas don't always show the differences between roles in crime science and investigation. It is important to distinguish between the work of a forensic scientist and a crime scene investigator, before making decisions about what type of job you might enjoy. The below charts explain the differences.

Forensic Scientist

Workplace: Most forensic scientists work in laboratories, where they analyze the evidence gathered by crime scene investigators.

Tools used: Forensic scientists use lab-based tools such as microscopes, spectrometry machines, and toxicology tools to carry out work.

Scope of work: It is possible to specialize in many different areas, from ballistics and fingerprint analysis through toxicology and DNA analysis.

Crime Scene Investigator

Workplace: Crime scene investigators go to crime scenes and collect evidence. They also analyze any evidence gathered at the crime scene.

Tools used: Crime scene investigators use in-the-field tools such as cameras, adhesive tapes, tweezers, collection bags, flashlights, blood-collection kits, and place cards.

Scope of work: Compared with a forensic scientist, the scope of this role is far narrower, but crime scene investigators could move on to other investigative fields, such as working for private investigation companies.

To pursue a career in forensic science or crime scene investigation, follow this simple flowchart.

Focus on your science subjects at school

Working in forensic science requires a strong scientific background, so concentrating on science topics at school is a must.

After school, earn an associate degree

Earning an associate degree applies to both forensic scientists and crime scene investigators, although some crime scene investigators enter the job without a degree, for example, they move into the work through the police force. After the degree stage, crime scene investigators will move into a job post. A forensic scientist will need to move on to further qualifications.

Earn a bachelor's degree

A forensic scientist will need a bachelor's degree for entry-level jobs. Often, employers will also ask for a master's degree too.

Choose a career area

At degree stage, forensic science students decide what area to specialize in, such as ballistics or autopsies, and complete courses that focus on those areas.

Apply for jobs

Once in a suitable role, valuable on-the-job training will be gained.

Earn further qualifications

Additional qualifications in specialist areas will add to your career potential, such as drug analysis, hair and fiber analysis, or fire damage analysis.

45

GLOSSARY

analysis the careful study of something

archaeologists people who study objects from the past

autopsies the examination of bodies after death to determine the causes of death

biomarkers measurements of biological processes

cells the smallest parts of all living things

committed carried out

contaminating making dirty or changing by adding a substance

convict to find a person guilty of a crime and to successfully put them in prison for that crime

database a usually large collection of data organized especially for quick search and retrieval of information

decayed rotted, or broken down

decomposed rotted, or broken down, into smaller parts

deoxyribonucleic acid (DNA) the unique code inside every human body cell that controls every element of how we look

disfigured changed and made difficult to recognize

evidence information, objects, or substances that are related to a crime

exhume to take a body out of its grave

fibers small pieces of cloth

forensic applying scientific knowledge to solve criminal and legal problems

forged made to look real but, in fact, is fake

genealogy related to the study of genes

genes the physical characteristics passed down from parents to their children

identify to figure out who someone is

lethal resulting in death

magnifying making very small things look bigger

microscope a tool used by scientists to look at things too small to see with the naked human eye

microscopic something that can be seen only with the aid of a microscope

mitochondrial relating to a tiny part of cells

origin where something or someone first came from

permission the act of allowing someone to do something

pollen a fine, powdery substance found in flowers

profile a description of someone based on information gathered about them

residue parts left behind after something is removed

samples small parts of something taken to examine them scientifically

scalpel a very sharp knife used to perform surgery

simulation an imitation of something

software computer programs that tell a computer what to do

suspect a person suspected of carrying out a crime

swabs absorbent materials used to collect DNA samples

touch DNA DNA that is passed onto someone or something else simply by touch

untampered not changed in any way

unwittingly accidentally, without knowing

validity how true or factually accurate something is

victim a person who has been injured, harmed, or killed by another person

witnesses people who saw something, such as a crime, take place

FIND OUT MORE

Books
Cooper, Chris. *Forensic Science: Discover the Fascinating Methods Scientists Use to Solve Crimes* (DK Eyewitness). DK Children, 2020.

Kortuem, Amy. *Blood Evidence* (Crime Solvers). Capstone Publishing, 2019.

Ross, Melissa. *Forensics for Kids: The Science and History of Crime Solving, With 21 Activities* (For Kids). Chicago Press Review, 2020.

Websites
Read the Civil Rights Cold Case Project website and discover how people tried to solve famous cold cases from the civil rights struggle at:
www.coldcases.org

Discover more about cold cases around the world at:
www.defrostingcoldcases.com

Find out more about DNA and how it works at:
https://kids.britannica.com/kids/article/DNA/390730

Publisher's note to educators and parents:
All the websites featured above have been carefully reviewed to ensure that they are suitable for students. However, many websites change often, and we cannot guarantee that a site's future contents will continue to meet our high standards of educational value. Please be advised that students should be closely monitored whenever they access the Internet.

INDEX

About the Author

Sarah Eason is an experienced children's book author who has written many science books for children. She loves watching crime-detective shows, and after researching and writing this book is more fascinated than ever by the world of cold cases and forensic science.